GERALD M. ROSEN, Ph.D., is chief psychologist at Providence Family Medical Center and in private practice, Seattle, Washington, He is also the author of *Don't Be Afraid: A Program for Overcoming Your Fears and Phobias.*

# THE RELAXATION BOOK

### An Illustrated Self-Help Program

GERALD ROSEN

*Illustrated by* JIM HAYS

A SPECTRUM BOOK

PRENTICE-HALL, INC., Englewood Cliffs, N.J. 07632

*Library of Congress Cataloging in Publication Data*
Rosen, Gerald M        date
   The relaxation book.

   (A Spectrum Book)
   Bibliography: p.
   1. Relaxation.    I.  Title.
RA785.R67        613.7′9        77-22675
ISBN 0-13-772210-9
ISBN 0-13-772202-8 pbk.

*TO MY PARENTS*

© 1977 by Gerald M. Rosen

A Spectrum Book

Printed in the United States of America

10   9   8   7   6   5   4   3   2   1

PRENTICE-HALL INTERNATIONAL, INC., *London*
PRENTICE-HALL OF AUSTRALIA PTY. LIMITED, *Sydney*
PRENTICE-HALL OF CANADA, LTD., *Toronto*
PRENTICE-HALL OF INDIA PRIVATE LIMITED, *New Delhi*
PRENTICE-HALL OF JAPAN, INC., *Tokyo*
PRENTICE-HALL OF SOUTHEAST ASIA PTE. LTD., *Singapore*
WHITEHALL BOOKS LIMITED, *Wellington, New Zealand*

# *Contents*

4

# *Credits*

Several people were instrumental in the development and publication of this book. Lynne Lumsden, editor of Spectrum Books, supported the concept of a self-help relaxation program and made the project possible. Significant help on the initial planning of the illustrations was provided by Glenda Utsey. Jim Hays completed the set of illustrations appearing in this edition, and I am glad we had the opportunity to work with each other. My wife, Betsy, provided valuable editorial assistance and reminded me to relax while I was writing.

To all of these people, thank you.

# 1

# Introductory Points

You may think we live in especially difficult times —and to some extent you're correct. Every day you face the responsibilities of getting an education, raising a family, managing a household, or advancing your career in a competitive world. In addition, numerous community and national issues demand your attention. On the same day you face exams or crying children or traffic jams, you also hear reports of unemployment, inflation, energy crises, and the threat of nuclear accidents.

You may indeed wonder if the pace of life has ever been as pressured as it is today. It may be hard to believe when *you* are feeling tense, but every period of history has had its difficulties; people have always been tense. Consider Dr. William Sadler's observation in 1914:

*As the strenuous life increases in city and country, there is an increased demand for relaxation . . . (and) escape from the clutch of the modern strenuous life.*

Before "modern strenuous life" and industrialized cities, people had other reasons for feeling tense. In fact, earlier periods of human history may have presented more difficult problems than today's pressured society. Although you may be troubled by the energy crisis or rising heat bills, your distant ancestors had worse things to worry about—many of them probably lived under the threat of freezing to death!

So people have always needed to relax. It should not be surprising, therefore, that various relaxation techniques

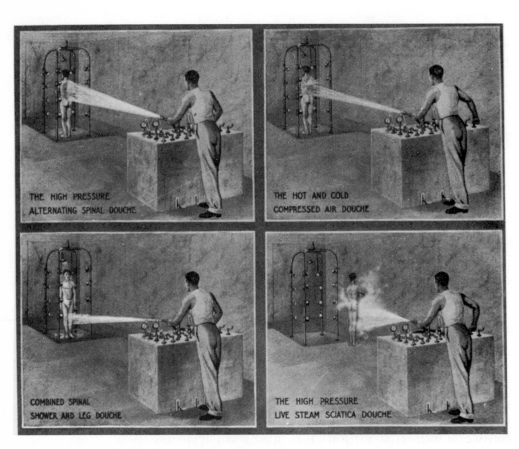

Hydrotherapy for nervous disorders.

Hot-air chambers were used in the early 1900s to treat a variety of physical and muscular ailments. In this photograph, a gas lamp is used as a source of heat to treat the muscles of the knee.

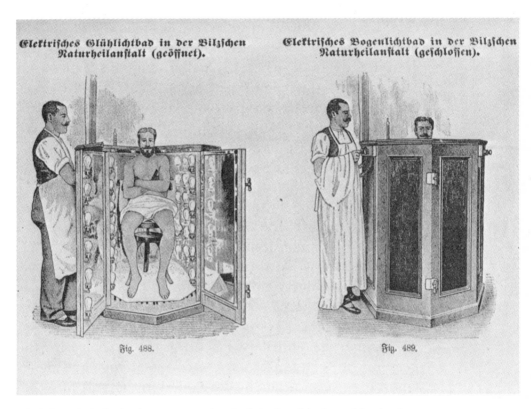

Elektrisches Glühlichtbad in der Bilzschen
Naturheilanstalt (geöffnet).

Elektrisches Bogenlichtbad in der Bilzschen
Naturheilanstalt (geschlossen).

Fig. 488.

Fig. 489.

The electric light bath was a mechanical device developed in the late 1800s. Much like today's saunas, the electric light bath was intended to remove tension from the body.

have been practiced throughout the centuries. Some of these methods, such as yoga, meditation, and body massage, were developed hundreds of years ago and are still practiced today. Other techniques have not been as long-lived. For example, when Dr. Sadler wrote his book in the early part of this century, elaborate mechanical devices and machines were being used to stimulate the body and relax the muscles. Most people living today have never heard of the "light eliminator bath" or the "high-pressured water douche"—two of the more popular techniques used by Dr. Sadler.

The most widely adopted modern method for coping with stress involves the use of drugs. One out of every 10 adults in the United States is considered to be using alcohol excessively. At the same time, the most prescribed drug in this country is the tranquilizer Valium. *Valium is more widely prescribed than penicillin, pain killers, or any other prescription drug you can name.*

Numerous alternatives to drugs are available for the person who feels tense. Various forms of yoga and meditation that were originally developed in the East have become popular in Western society. Hypnosis, auto hypnosis, autogenic training, and a variety of breathing exercise programs are also available to the tense individual. Other treatment experiences include T-groups, primal scream, transactional analysis, psychoanalysis, EST, behavior modification, biofeedback, and growth workshops.

The person who is tense and wants to relax is faced with a truly confusing situation. How does one choose, among so many treatments, the specific procedure that is most appropriate to his or her problem?

It is possible to reduce some of the confusion by drawing a basic distinction between many of today's treatments. As it turns out, most treatments do not teach skills directly related to body relaxation. Thus primal scream, EST, transactional analysis, psychoanalysis, and many other popular treatments may be useful, but they do not really teach methods for reducing physical tension and increasing body relaxation. Instead, these treatments focus on the analysis or expression of your feelings.

A number of modern treatments do teach relaxation skills. The most popular of these include transcendental meditation, zen and yoga, autogenic training, progressive relaxation, and hypnosis with suggestions for deep relaxation. Which one of these approaches is best? Based on current work by professionals, it appears that you need not worry about this question. Evidently, all of them are useful. In fact, all of today's relaxation programs probably accomplish the exact same thing!

This last conclusion was the basic point in Dr. Herbert Benson's book, *The Relaxation Response*, in which he discussed the results of research conducted at Beth Israel Hospital in New York City. The various relaxation procedures that Dr. Benson and his colleagues studied always led to the same physical reactions—lowered blood pressure and heart rate, slowed respiration, lowered oxygen consumption, and reduced muscle tension. These findings suggested to Dr. Benson the presence of a natural and innate relaxation response. He concluded that all of today's popular relaxation programs are *equally* successful in helping a person achieve that response.

Benson indicated four procedural steps involved in each of the programs he studied. He reasoned that whether one is meditating, practicing autogenic training, or working on progressive relaxation, the relaxation response is produced by the following:

1. A quiet environment.
2. A comfortable position.
3. A mental device (some thought or object upon which to focus your attention).
4. A passive attitude whereby distractions are ignored and attention remains focused on the mental device.

The basic procedures for bringing on the relaxation response have one very real limitation—they require that

you get away from the regular world if you want to experience deep relaxation. To practice transcendental meditation, autogenic training, yoga, or Dr. Benson's basic four steps, you need to assume a comfortable position in a quiet environment, and you need to ignore all distracting influences.

So, the natural question is, "When can I do that?" It usually isn't possible to leave work when your tension starts to build. In a traffic jam, you can't assume a comfortable position and ignore the distractions around you. Evidently, popular relaxation programs can help during special sessions at home, but they leave you empty-handed when regular daily tensions occur. In this way, yoga, meditation, and other relaxation procedures are similar to one of the oldest remedies for tension—the vacation. During a vacation you temporarily get away from it all and "leave your tensions behind." Eventually, you must return to your regular daily routine, and so your vacation comes to an end. The same thing is true with relaxation programs. After your special 10- or 20- minute sessions, you are back in the real world—studying at the library, driving to work, cleaning the house, or taking care of some other concern.

Many people report that short relaxation sessions are helpful in getting them through the entire day. And you may have noticed that you really do feel better that first week you are back from vacation. But, ideally, a program for tension problems should teach you two things.

## THE BASIC RELAXATION RESPONSE

A relaxation program should teach you how to produce the basic relaxation response so that you can eliminate tension from your body and enjoy a *deep* sense of relaxation. This response could be produced once, twice, or several times a day depending on how often you need it and how often you could get away to a comfortable and quiet setting.

## ADDITIONAL RELAXATION SKILLS

In addition to the relaxation response, you should learn relaxation skills that can be used throughout the day. Developing these skills will allow you to minimize muscle tension almost anywhere. Even in stressful situations that cannot be avoided, you can better cope and remain more relaxed.

## YOUR RELAXATION PROGRAM

This program can help you to accomplish the two goals just described. You can learn to produce the relaxation response during practice sessons at home, and you can learn to use basic relaxation skills throughout the day. To decide if these goals are appropriate to *your* particular situation, there are two issues you should consider.

The first issue concerns your reasons for wanting to relax—and there are dozens of possibilities. Learning to relax can help you to deal with daily tensions so you will feel more rested and will use your energy more efficiently during the day. Relaxation is also useful in treating common physical complaints, such as insomnia or tension headaches. Many investigators feel that relaxation training also helps people with high blood pressure.

A complete list of problems that have been treated successfully with relaxation programs would probably fill several pages. Yet it would be wrong to think of this (or any other) relaxation program as a cure-all for every ailment. Thus learning to relax can increase your comfort in everyday situations, but it will not eliminate strong fears and phobias. It is one thing to feel tense when working all day at a desk. It is another matter when a person actually avoids work and stays at home because of a fear or phobia.

In a similar way, relaxation programs are not going to cure a real physical ailment. Headaches caused by tension may be helped by relaxing; but headaches resulting from a tumor require different care. Like considerations apply to sleep disturbances as these can be caused by tension or a variety of medical problems.

To decide if this relaxation program is really for you, consider the following:

1. This program is useful if you want to reduce tension, learn to relax, and better cope with environmental stress.

2. If you have a physical complaint that you believe is the result of tension, check it out with your physician. *Do not rely solely on your own diagnosis.* Also, if tension is not related to particular situations or people, there must be something causing your discomfort—and it could be a medical problem. Thyroid dysfunctions, hypoglycemia, and other medical disorders often account for emotional problems. Remember this if you feel unusual tension and cannot explain your reactions. In such instances, consult with your physican. Your doctor can evaluate your medical situation and then give you the go ahead to work on this program.

3. If instead of tension problems you have a strong fear or phobia, consider using a different type of program. One that I have written is *Don't Be Afraid: A Program For Overcoming Your Fears And Phobias* (Prentice-Hall, 1976). Other programs for fear reduction also have been published. Whatever program you choose, be certain that it is right for your situation.

4. If your problem is primarily concerned with sleep disturbances, you may also want to read *How to Sleep Better: A Drug-free Program for Overcoming Insomnia* by Thomas Coates and Carl Thoresen (Prentice-Hall, 1977.)

After deciding if your interest in this program is for the right reasons, you need to consider the second issue—how motivated you really are when it comes to conducting your own treatment. Learning to relax is a skill: and like any other skill, it takes practice to learn it well. Of course, practice does not have to be tedious or overly long. Two half-hour sessions each week, plus daily practice sessions of 10 to 15 minutes, are all that is required. The entire program takes most people only three to six weeks to master. And that surely is a short time to learn how to relax.

Still the program does require motivation and a real commitment. So you should ask yourself two questions:

Am I Really Concerned About a Tension Problem?
Am I Sufficiently Motivated To Work On This Porgram?

If you answer yes to both questions, then read on—this book is for you. In the following chapters you will learn how to self-administer an effective relaxation program. You will learn the basic *relaxation response* as well as everyday *relaxation skills*.

**HOW TO APPROACH YOUR WORK**

If you were working with a therapist in a professional office, you would certainly follow the treatment program step-by-step. Only after you had successfully completed the first part of the procedures would your therapist present the second part. You should use your written relaxation program in the same way—by letting it systematically

16

guide you through the procedures—just as a therapist would. Be sure to follow the instructions in their proper order, one step at a time.

You should also structure your program as if you were seeing a therapist in an office. Experience with people who use self-administered programs suggests that this is the most critical issue. Consider the following situations to see why.

*Situation 1:* Sarah has an appointment with a very busy doctor for Friday afternoon at four. She has been waiting for some time to see this doctor, and she really feels she needs some help to learn how to relax. Earlier in the week, a man whom Sarah has been wanting to see calls her. He suggests that they go out on Friday for a late afternoon movie and then dinner. What does Sarah do?

Does she say she can't make the date because she has a very important appointment, but she would like to get together some other time? Or does Sarah figure that she can get another appointment with the doctor later, and say yes to the date?

*Situation 2:* Sarah has scheduled a session for herself to work on her self-administered relaxation program. She has been waiting all week to hold this session, and she really feels she needs to work on her tension problems. The session is scheduled for late Friday afternoon since that is her only free time this week. A man whom Sarah would like to see suggests going to a late afternoon movie and dinner on Friday. Again, what does Sarah do?

What Sarah is likely to do in the above two situations is all too clear. And so you can see the problem. When you have an appointment with a busy doctor, you tend to be responsible and keep it. When you don't have this outside support, it is more difficult to stick to your plans.

To help you treat your sessions in a responsible manner, it is a good idea to schedule regular meeting times. These times then can be treated as doctor appointments. If you are ill or can't make a session for some other good reason, show yourself the same courtesy you would extend to a doctor—reschedule for a new time.

Before starting your program, decide when to meet regularly with yourself. You will want to choose two times during the week that are likely to remain convenient over the next several weeks. And it is a good idea to allow a few days between your sessions. If one session is on Monday, your next session could be on Thursday or Friday, not on Tuesday. Also, your first session will be almost a full hour long. After that, the sessions will never take more than 30 minutes.

When you have decided on convenient times, write them down for the next few weeks on a calendar. This will help you to remember your appointments, just as if you were seeing a doctor.

## HOW TO ASSESS YOUR TENSION

Every day of your program you should ask yourself, "How *tense* was I today?" In this way you can carefully identify where, when, and how you experience tension.

You can also observe changes in your reactions as you develop relaxation skills. Then, in Chapter 4 you will be asked, "How *relaxed* are you now?" Your daily observations during the program will help you to assess your progress and evaluate what you have learned.

It helps to keep a record or diary of daily tension reactions to assess your feelings systematically. If this seems like a chore, try to change your attitude, become more interested. After all, do you really know how tense you feel on Mondays as compared to Wednesdays? Are those weekday evenings that much worse than the ones on the weekends? Do you have trouble getting to sleep on days when a math class or a business meeting is held, or does your insomnia have more to do with your home life? Most people cannot answer these questions until they formally assess their tension reactions on a daily basis. Even people who *think* they know the answers can be surprised when they look carefully at real "data."

So be a little curious about your feelings and tension levels. Shift into a new role and adopt a new attitude. Instead of being at the mercy of your tension, become an "objective observer" of your reactions—and get ready to see those reactions change.

How you keep a diary will greatly depend on the nature of your reactions, the situations that make you tense, and your particular goals. Tension can take many forms. Some people become tense in only one or two situations; others feel on edge throughout the day. While one person can become snappy and irritable when tense, another will withdraw into silence. Tension can cause you to feel light-headed, develop a rapid heartbeat, or perspire heavily. You may experience muscle tightness in your face and neck; a friend may become tense in the legs or stomach. No two people are exactly the same when it comes to their experiences of tension.

Take a few minutes to think about your reactions, and then study the sample assessment forms on the following pages. The first form is useful if you want to track physical complaints or problem situations that relate to your tension reactions. The second assessment form can be used to monitor general feelings of tension that you have during an entire day. This form is useful when your tension is not clearly associated with easily identified situations. As you read about the two types of forms, decide which one will be most suited to your particular needs.

**Assessment Form for Physical Complaints and Problem Situations**

Look at the sample assessment form on page 23. This form can be used to evaluate daily tension reactions associated with physical complaints, such as headaches, insomnia, stiff neck, or back pain. It is also useful if your tension is associated with particular situations or specific times of the day.

Whenever a physical complaint or problem situation occurs, this is what to do:

1. Indicate how uncomfortable you feel. How severe is your headache? How tense is the pain in your back?

**20**

How upset did the situation make you feel? Rate the severity of your discomfort on a 10-point scale. Let 0 represent no tension, or Totally Relaxed, and let 10 represent severe tension, or As Uncomfortable As I Could Ever Be. All numbers between 0 and 10 represent subjective units of discomfort—the larger the number, the more units of discomfort, and the more uncomfortable you feel.

2. In addition to a discomfort rating, it is useful to note other features of your reactions. If you have a headache, record how long it lasts and what medications you take to relieve the pain. If you have a sleep disturbance, record in the morning how long it took to get to sleep the night before, how many times you awakened during the night, or how early you arose in the morning. If a difficult situation has occurred, note those aspects that have made you tense.

3. Whenever you associate a particular situation or individual with your tension reactions, consider this very important point: In many cases you will want to relax and better cope with difficult situations. These are times when something is "getting to you" more than it should. For example, consider Problem 2 on the sample form. It seems reasonable that a mother would want to improve her coping skills and learn to relax when driving her child to school. *But*—in other situations, it may be that someone else should change—*not you!*

Consider Problem 3 on the sample form where it appears that the children's behavior is out of control. Rather than mother learning to relax, it could be that she should better discipline her children. A more forceful example of this same point is the wife who has to cope with an overdemanding, dominating husband. Add to the husband's annoying behavior a drinking problem and the wife will have every reason to feel tense. It would be unreasonable to suggest that a woman should accept an assaultive, alcoholic husband and simply relax away her tension.

*Remember, if someone else does something that makes you tense, it may not be appropriate to relax and accept it. It may be more appropriate to assert yourself and ask for a change in the other person. Always ask yourself this question: Am I being overly tense and do I need to relax: or does someone else in this situation need to do some changing?*

4. At the end of each week you can assess your general reactions by averaging the daily information. To do this, add up the total number of headaches, aspirins, units of discomfort, or whatever you are tracking. Then divide by the number of days in a week, or by the number of physical complaints or problem situations that occurred.

The weekly averages you obtain can be used to see how things are changing from one week to the next. For example, the first assessment form shows the daily records of a woman who averaged one headache per day (Problem 1). This was easily determined by dividing the total number of headaches (7) by the number of days in a week. The woman's headaches typically lasted 1 hour (a total of 7 hours divided by 7 headaches), and they typically caused 7 units of discomfort (a total of 49 discomfort units divided by 7 headaches). By the third week of her relaxation

# Assessment Form for Physical Complaints and Problem Situations

| WEEK ___ | PROBLEM 1 Headaches | | PROBLEM 2 Driving Johnny to school | | PROBLEM 3 Preparing dinner | |
|---|---|---|---|---|---|---|
| | Rating | Comments | Rating | Comments | Rating | Comments |
| MONDAY Feb. 14 | 8 | Started 9 am. Lasted 1 hour. Took 2 aspirins | 6 | Johnny had got to bed late, was irritable in the morning | 8 | Got a late start — trouble with kids after school |
| TUESDAY 15 | 5<br>7 | 7:30 am, ½ hr, 1 aspirin 6 pm, 1 hr, 1 aspirin | 7 | Johnny was OK but traffic was bad | 8 | Trouble with kids |
| WEDNESDAY 16 | 3 | 9 pm, ½ hour, no medicine | 4 | Light traffic | 7 | Bob home late — kids acting up |
| THURSDAY 17 | | | 4 | Light traffic | 8 | Trouble with kids |
| FRIDAY 18 | 9 | 5 pm, 1 hr, 2 aspirins | 8 | Heavy traffic | 4 | Bob home early — kids out of the way |
| SATURDAY 19 | 10<br>7 | 3 pm, 2 hrs, 2½ aspirins 7:30 pm, 1 hr, 2 aspirins | | | 2 | Kids tired from day at park—no problem |
| SUNDAY 20 | | | | | 4 | Kids restless |

AVERAGES: Headaches—1 per day. They lasted 1 hour and my rating averages 7.0. Averaged 1.5 aspirins per headache.

Driving to school every week-day. Average rating was 5.8. Seems to be a function of traffic.

Preparing dinner — tension high: almost every day average rating was 5.9. Kids' behavior is responsible.

program, this woman may still have 1 headache every day, but at that point they may last only 30 minutes and cause an average discomfort rating of 4. Or, she could continue to have hour-long headaches and experience 7 units of discomfort, but her headaches may no longer occur every day.

How your tension reactions change can be evaluated by looking at the weekly averages computed from your daily records.

5. Do not keep a diary on everything that troubles you, since you can observe only just so much at any given time. Instead, limit yourself to no more than three events. You can track three physical complaints, three situations, or any combination of these (for example, two physical complaints and one problem situation). Also avoid choosing your three most difficult problems. They may be the slowest to change, and it is rewarding to observe improvement early in your program. So, keep track of at least one mild or less severe complaint.

**Assessment Form for General Feelings of Tension**

You may not associate specific situations or particular physical complaints with your tension reactions. In that case, use an assessment form like the following one. Notice how this form differs from the one previously discussed. In the far left-hand column is space for you to write in two-hour blocks of time. Then there is room under each

# Assessment Form for Recording General Feelings of Tension

WEEK ___

Write in this left-hand column, two-hour time blocks.

| TIME/DAY | Mon. | Tue. | Wed. | Thur. | Fri. | Sat. | Sun. | COMMENTS | AVERAGES: |
|---|---|---|---|---|---|---|---|---|---|
| 8-10 am | 4 | 5 | 3 | 4 | 3 | 1 | 1 | | 3.8 |
| 10am to noon | 1 | 3 | 1 | 7 | 3 | 2 | 1 | Thursday (7): Called car mechanic | 2.6 |
| Noon to 2pm | 2 | 3 | 2 | 3 | 4 | 3 | 1 | | 2.6 |
| 2-4pm | 4 | 4 | 5 | 4 | 4 | 2 | 1 | | 3.4 |
| 4-6pm | 6 | 8 | 4 | 8 | 9 | 2 | 2 | Monday (6): kids home and housecleaning wasn't done; Tuesday (8): long lines at grocery store; Thursday (8), Friday (9): housecleaning not done | 5.6 |
| 6-8pm | 4 | 3 | 3 | 5 | 6 | 3 | 3 | Friday (6): tense about entertaining guests | 3.9 |
| 8-10pm | 2 | 3 | 1 | 3 | 3 | 4 | 2 | | 2.6 |
| 10pm to midnight | 2 | 1 | 1 | 2 | 2 | 3 | 1 | | 2.2 |
| AVERAGES: | 3.1 | 4.1 | 2.7 | 4.5 | 4.2 | 2.7 | 1.7 | | |

day (Monday = M, Tuesday = T, and so on) for you to rate how tense you felt during the time periods. Your ratings should be based on the highest amount of tension felt during each two-hour interval. For example, if a phone call upsets you and you feel 8 units of discomfort, write an 8 on your sheet even if you generally felt only 4 units of discomfort during that period. Under the "comments" section, explain the particular situation that caused the high rating.

Take time to make additional comments only when your tension ratings are high. These comments can then help to identify specific situations that relate to your tension reactions. If specific situations are identified, switch over to the first assessment form.

As long as you are unable to relate specific situations to your tension reactions, continue to use the second assessment form. At the end of each week, average your discomfort ratings for each day and for each two-hour block of time. To compute daily averages, simply add all your ratings on a given day and divide by the number of ratings. In the present example, 8 ratings were made on Monday. The total for these ratings was 25, so the average rating for Monday was 3.1. To compute an average for each time block, add your ratings across the days and divide the total by the number of ratings. The 7 ratings from the sample form for the 4—6 p.m. time block totaled 39, so the average rating was 5.6.

The averages you compute can help you to see if particular days, or particular hours in a day, are more difficult than others. In the present example, it appears that weekends are somewhat more relaxing than weekdays, and the most difficult time of the day is when the kids are home and housecleaning chores need to be finished.

During the weeks of your program, notice how your average tension ratings change. This will be particularly interesting when difficult time periods are considered.

One last point. Despite its usefulness, some people find that keeping a daily record of tension reactions is simply too much work. If this should turn out to be the way you feel, do not give up on the entire program. The assessment forms provide a useful tool, but *they are not essential to a successful program.* Remember—everyone should try the assessment forms, but if they don't work out for you do not become overly discouraged. Instead, drop that part of your program and continue to work on the relaxation exercises discussed in Chapters 2 and 3.

## WHAT TO DO NOW

In the back of this book you will find copies of the different assessment forms just described. Take a few minutes to consider your tension reactions and then decide which form is best suited to your needs. Use the form you chose to record your tension reactions on a daily basis, and try to do this throughout the course of your program.

Plan to start your recording tomorrow morning. For today, stop now and put your book aside. Wait until your first regularly scheduled meeting to begin work on the next chapter, in which you will learn the rules of your program. Be sure to have a full hour set aside for this session because there is a good deal of new information to absorb. After your first session, you will begin regular 30-minute practice sessions. In less than one week's time, you will be learning how to relax.

Wait until your first regularly scheduled session to begin the next chapter. Remember to start your diary tomorrow by using the assessment forms in the back of this book.

# 2

# Learn
# To Relax

You are now ready to learn how to relax. During today's session, carefully study all of the instructions in this chapter. The session may be a long one because of the amount of new material. If necessary, you may want to spend part of your second session finishing the instructions.

There are three important points to keep in mind as you begin this program. First, do not expect "immediate results" and, second, do not be overly concerned about your rate of progress. Some people finish the program in three weeks, others take six weeks or more. As long as you work at the procedures and practice them conscientiously, you will enjoy feelings of deep relaxation by the end of the program. So take it easy. Trying too hard and forcing yourself to relax will only make you tense!

A third point to remember is that the instructions in this chapter teach you basic skills that you practice at home. After you can relax at home, you will extend your skills and learn to relax in many everyday situations. But that will take time and you should remain patient during the next few weeks.

## A BASIC PRINCIPLE

Your first goal in this program is to learn what the opposing feelings of tension and relaxation are really like. One of the best ways to identify these feelings is alternately to tense and relax various muscle groups. To illustrate how this works, you can practice a demonstration trial now. Take your dominant hand (if you are right-handed, use your right hand; if left-handed, use your left hand) and make a loose fist without applying any pressure. Continue to read these instructions. When you come across the word NOW in capital letters following this paragraph, slightly tighten your fist and notice the tension you produce. You will probably feel tension in your knuckles, in your fingers, and in other parts of your arm. Remember not to tense so hard that it hurts. Just make your fist tight enough to feel *slight* increases in tension. When you make the fist, hold it for about five to seven seconds. It will take about that long to read the instructions. Then, when you see the word RELAX in capital letters, remove the tension by quickly opening your hand and relaxing the muscles. Get ready by making yourself comfortable. Have your arm resting on the chair you are in and . . .

**NOW**

Slightly tighten your fist and hold it. Do you feel tension in your fingers? In your knuckles? Does the tension spread to your wrist and forearm? Briefly study the tension in your hand. Then, let yourself . . .

**RELAX**

Let go of the tension and rest your hand comfortably on the chair or in your lap. Experience the tension you purposefully put into your muscles as it leaves the tense areas. Study the changing sensations.

It doesn't matter if the effects you just felt were large or small. And it doesn't even matter if your hand still feels a little tense. The purpose of the demonstration is simply to illustrate the basic procedural components for physical relaxation training.

Note that during the *tension phases* of your program you learn to identify specific points where muscle tension exists for you. For example, when you make a fist, you may find that tension builds in your knuckles, in the tips of your fingers, or in your wrist. You may feel tension in the palm of your hand . . . then again, you may not. Purposefully tensing muscles gives you a chance to study where your muscles get tight.

Tensing muscles also lets you feel what it is like when tension leaves your body during the *relaxation phases* of your program. As your muscles relax, you can contrast the opposing feelings of tension and relaxation. With practice, you will learn to gain control over this process and extend feelings of relaxation throughout your muscle groups.

This then is the basic principle for the beginning of your relaxation program:

> *By alternately tensing and relaxing muscles, you learn to identify feelings of tension and substitute comfortable feelings of relaxation.*

## THE MUSCLE GROUPS

To study the opposing feelings of tension and relaxation effectively, you should focus on one area of your body at a time. In that way you can better concentrate on particular muscle groups and learn how each part of your body reacts. This program divides your body into 15 individual areas that can be combined to form four major groups.

*Major Group 1:*
    a. Dominant hand and forearm

    b. Dominant biceps

    c. Nondominant hand and forearm

    d. Nondominant biceps

*Major Group 2:*
    a. Forehead

    b. Cheeks and nose

    c. Jaws

    d. Lips and tongue

    e. Neck and throat

*Major Group 3:*
    a. Shoulders and upper back

    b. Chest

    c. Stomach

*Major Group 4:*
    a. Thighs and buttocks

    b. Calves

    c. Feet

To study the opposing feelings of tension and relaxation, you need to know how each muscle group is tensed; and some muscles in your program can be tensed in more than one way. The following pages describe various methods, and you should see how you most prefer to tense your muscles. To do this, briefly create a *very slight* amount of tension in each muscle group as it is discussed.

One factor that will influence the tension methods you prefer is the place where you intend to practice. For example, how you tense your calves or feet will greatly depend on whether you are sitting or lying down. So you should now give some thought to where you plan to hold your regular sessions. Choose a place that is private, comfortable, quiet, and free from distractions. Pick a place that allows you to close a door so that family, friends, or pets will not interrupt in the middle of a session.

Most people like to practice their relaxation exercises while sitting in a large, comfortable, overstuffed chair. Ideally, your chair should have a high back so that it supports your neck and head. If you do not have an adequate chair in your home, you can practice while lying on your bed. Or, you can pile pillows at the head of your bed, then sit up on the bed with your feet straight out and your back, neck, and head supported by the pillows.

Decide where you want to practice. Then take this book and actually go to that location. Get yourself comfortable, and continue reading.

Once you are comfortable, carefully read the following pages and see how you can tense the muscles included in your program. When more than one method is described, decide on the one you want to use.

On page 42, there is space for you to record how you choose to tense each muscle group. As you work through the instructions, take the time to write down your decisions. In that way you will have a convenient reference list that can be used during practice sessions.

Do not confuse the tension exercises you are about to practice with actual relaxation training. For the time being, you are simply going to rehearse various procedures for the tension phases of your program. You do not *alternately* tense and relax the various groups until later, and the rules for doing that are not discussed until the next instructional section. You will then learn how to "self-instruct" yourself during practice sessions. Problems you may encounter and how you should schedule your sessions also will be clarified. Remember, each section is to be studied one step at a time.

# HOW TO TENSE EACH OF YOUR MUSCLE GROUPS

INSTRUCTIONS: Write in the spaces below the method you most prefer for tensing a particular muscle group. When you have listed all the muscles, you can use this page as a convenient reference list.

Major Group 1: HANDS AND ARMS

a. Dominant hand and forearm ................................................................

b. Dominant biceps ................................................................

(Note: The nondominant hand and forearm and the nondominant biceps are practiced in a similar manner.)

Major Group 2: HEAD, FACE, AND THROAT

a. Forehead ................................................................

b. Cheeks and nose ................................................................

c. Jaws ................................................................

d. Lips and tongue ................................................................

e. Neck and throat ................................................................

Major Group 3: SHOULDERS, CHEST, AND STOMACH

a. Shoulders and upper back ................................................................

b. Chest ................................................................

c. Stomach ................................................................

Major Group 4: LEGS AND FEET

a. Thighs and buttocks ................................................................

b. Calves ................................................................

c. Feet ................................................................

## Hands and Forearms

The dominant hand and forearm include the muscle groups that you previously tensed by making a fist and holding it tight. This is an easy group to practice, but be sure to consider the many points where tension can build. There are five individual fingers, the various sections of your fingers (tips, knuckles), the palm of your hand, the back of your hand, your wrist, and the forearm muscles. Consider each of these points when you make a fist and tighten your muscles.

Your nondominant hand and forearm are tensed in the same manner.

 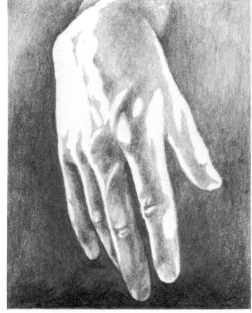

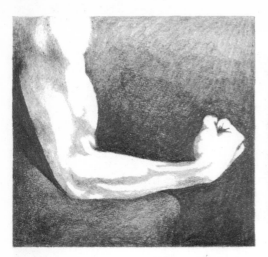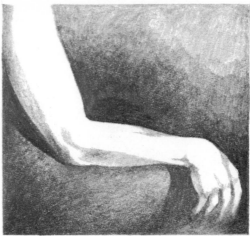

**Biceps**

This is the part of the upper arm that bulges when you "make a muscle" like the "strong man" on the beach. Tense this group by keeping your arm flat on the chair with the palm of your hand facing up. Push with your elbow down into the arm of the chair, creating tension in your biceps. If this method is not effective for you, bend your arm at the elbow so that your hand faces toward your shoulder and your elbow is free from the arm of the chair. Then apply what is called a *counterforce*. To do this, try touching your shoulder with your hand, at the same time opposing this movement. Your hand will seem frozen in midair by the two opposing forces. This is exactly what Superman and other comic book heroes do when showing off their arm muscles.

Your dominant and nondominant biceps are tensed in the same manner. Naturally, if you are not practicing in a chair, the second method is preferable.

**Forehead**

Tension is often felt most strongly in the facial muscles. Every time you talk, smile, frown, or cry, you are using the muscles in your face. So pay especially close attention to the next five muscles in Major Group 2.

To tense the muscles in your forehead, try lifting your eyebrows high as if you wanted them to touch the top of your head. An alternative method is to frown, or "knit your brows."

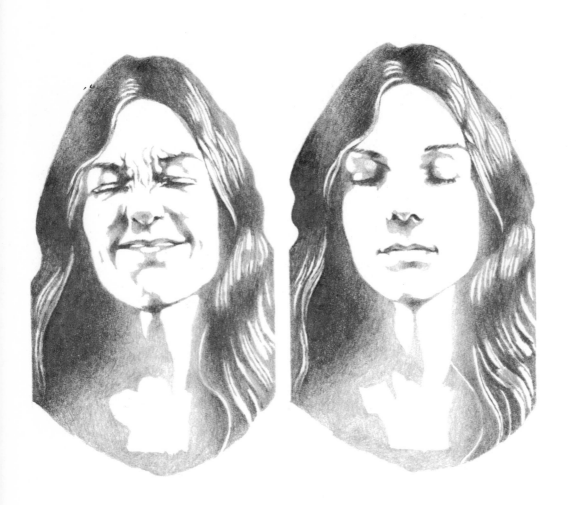

### Cheeks and Nose

Squint your eyes and wrinkle your nose. Don't be afraid of making funny faces when you practice!

46

## Jaws

These muscles can be tensed by clenching your teeth together hard and pulling back the corners of your mouth.

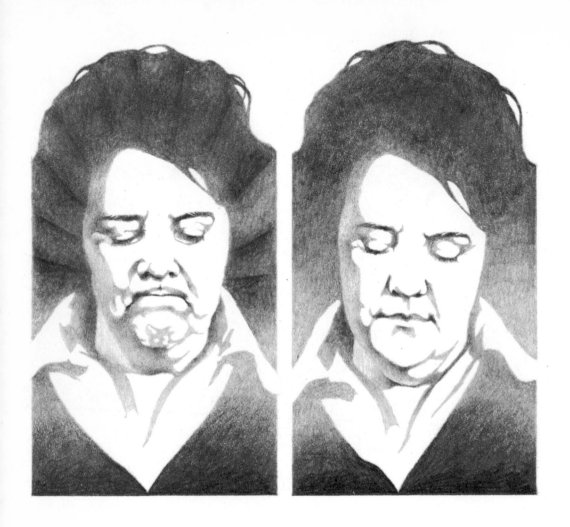

## Lips and Tongue

With teeth separated, press your lips together, and then press your tongue against the roof of your mouth.

### Neck and Throat

Pull your chin down as if trying to touch it to your chest. Now apply a counterpressure, or opposing force, to stop your chin. An alternative method, if your chair is tall enough or if you are propped up against pillows, is to press your head back.

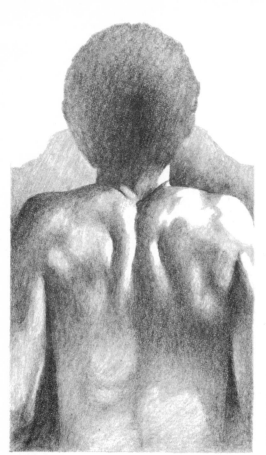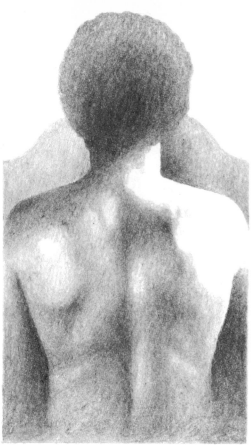

## Shoulders and Upper Back

Pull your shoulders up as if they were being held by strings attached to the ceiling. If you are lying down, pull them up toward your ears. Then arch them back as if trying to touch your shoulder blades together.

**Chest**

To tense the muscles in your chest, take a deep breath and hold it for five to seven seconds. Exhale in an even and smooth manner. Do not breathe out so slowly that you exert effort holding air in, and do not breathe so fast that you push air out. Exhale at whatever rate requires the *least* effort.

Practicing the muscles in your chest, and learning to exhale in a smooth and even manner, is an important key to a successful program. Controlled breathing can increase general levels of relaxation throughout your body. Controlled breathing also serves as a *connecting link* that helps to relax your mind and body. Later in the program you will see how this works. For the time being, remember this extremely important point: *Exhaling is the relaxing phase of the breathing cycle.*

**Stomach**

The stomach muscles are most easily tensed either by making your stomach hard, pulling your stomach in and holding it tight, or pushing your stomach out.

**Thighs and Buttocks**

There is no illustration for this muscle group, but your thighs and buttocks can be tensed by consciously trying to tighten them while pressing your heels into the ground. An alternative counterforce method involves pressing your knees toward each other, at the same time applying pressure to keep them apart. When doing this, pretend that a rubber ball is between your knees and preventing them from touching each other.

If neither of these methods creates tension, try lifting your legs straight out in front of you.

 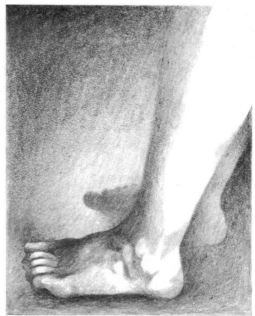

**Calves**

Point your toes up toward your head. Or, point your
toes down away from your head.

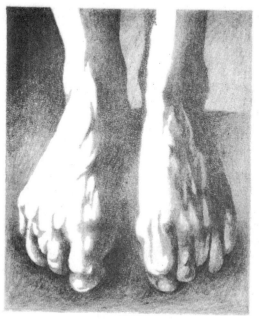 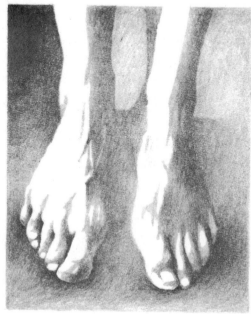

**Feet**

These muscles can easily cramp, and you want to avoid that. Be certain that you tense these muscles only very slightly. Also, use a short 3-second period for holding the tension.

Tense your feet by pointing them slightly down, turning them inward, and curling your toes.

Take a few minutes to study your list of muscle groups. Try to become familiar with each of the areas and the methods used to tense them. Do this before going on to the next set of instructions.

## HOW TO PRACTICE EACH MUSCLE GROUP

Now that you know the muscle groups involved in your program, let's look at how you should practice them. First, you want to work on the muscle groups in their listed order. Start with your hand and arm muscles, then practice your facial muscles, and so on down the list. As you work on the muscles in the listed order, be sure to follow these eight rules:

*Rule 1:* When first practicing a particular group, tense the appropriate muscles for a 5-to 7-second period. The only exceptions are your feet and other muscles that may have a tendency to cramp. In that case, decrease the tension period to about 3 seconds.

*Rule 2:* Do not tense your muscles so hard that they hurt. Instead, use the smallest amount of tension necessary to identify each distinct point of muscle tightness. One of the most common errors that people make in this program is to use too much tension. Be certain that you don't do this.

*Rule 3:* After the 5-to 7-second tension period, actively reduce tension by quickly releasing your hold on the muscles. Then, for a period of 20 to 30 seconds, spend your time consciously extending feelings of relaxation throughout your muscles. During this period, concentrate on the contrast between tension and relaxation. Remember that some muscle fibers may still be tensed even when you start to feel relaxed. Relaxing is an active process of undoing tension, and you want to extend this process as far as possible.

*Rule 4:* Each muscle group should be practiced at least twice. If after two trials there is no residual tension and your muscles feel relaxed, you can start working with the next muscle group on your list. If tension remains, continue to practice the same group for as many as five trials in a single session. Then stop and go to the next group.

*Rule 5:* When you tense a muscle, try to keep the involvement of adjacent areas to a minimum. Sometimes this can be difficult. For example, tensing the arm often leads to a tightening up of the fist as well. There is nothing wrong with this as long as you focus attention only on the particular muscle group you are practicing.

*Rule 6:* When you finish all the muscles in a major group, take some time to review them and relax more fully. For instance, after you have practiced your hands and arms (Major Group 1), spend a minute or two extending relaxation further and further. Let yourself experience even greater levels of comfort in these muscles. After this "review break," you can start the individual muscles in the next major group.

*Rule 7:* Throughout the relaxation phases of the procedure, let yourself enjoy the relaxing effects of exhaling evenly and smoothly. Exhaling is the relaxing phase of the breathing cycle. It is a good feeling, and, with practice, you can learn to take full advantage of it. As you exhale, think relaxing expressions to yourself or words like *calm, peaceful, serene.*

*Rule 8:* Always practice with your eyes closed. This eliminates distractions and lets you focus your full attention on the changing sensations in each muscle.

## Let's Review the Rules

First, practice each muscle group in its listed order by alternately tensing (5 to 7 seconds) and relaxing (20 to 30 seconds) the muscle at least twice. If a group remains tense, you can practice it up to five times in a single session. When you have finished all the muscles in a major group, take some time to extend relaxation to deeper and deeper levels. To do this, take advantage of relaxing expressions and the effects of exhaling evenly and smoothly. As you practice, keep your eyes closed and focus your attention on just one muscle group at a time.

After a review break, continue on to the muscles in the next major group and practice them in the same way. Follow this procedure for about 30 minutes during each session, completing as many of the muscle groups as you can.

## HOW TO INSTRUCT YOURSELF

To teach yourself relaxation skills effectively, you need to know appropriate expressions for tensing and relaxing. In a clinical setting, a therapist would take you through the procedures and tell you at each point what to do. At home, you are your own therapist and you will need to instruct yourself. A sample set of instructions follows to illustrate how you might tell yourself what to do. These instructions have been written for the forehead muscles, but similar expressions could be used for any of the muscle groups.

*I'm going to relax my entire body to the best of my ability. I'm settling back now and getting comfortable. I'm ready to begin practicing, and I'm going to tighten up my forehead, NOW . . . keep my forehead wrinkled . . . tight . . . experience the tension in my muscles and now . . . RELAX . . . throw away the tightness and do the opposite of tensing . . . relax . . . let go of all the tension and spread the feelings of relaxation all over . . . experience the contrast between tension and relaxation . . . OK, once again, NOW tense my forehead . . . that's right, put tension back into my muscles and again study the tension . . . hold the tension another few seconds and now RELAX again . . . enjoy the contrast . . . let me see how far I can extend the process . . . letting the relaxation spread over my forehead . . . relaxing . . . relaxing.*

Read the above example again. Practice creating an initial sense of tension and then let the relaxation instructions create a lazy calm feeling of restfulness.

Professionals use a number of standard phrases during relaxation training programs. These expressions can be used interchangeably with any individual group.

### Tension Phrases

Feel the muscles pull . . . hold it.
Tighten my muscles.
Pay attention to these muscles, identify the tension.
Study (attend to) the tension.
Notice where the tightness is for me.
Put tension into my muscles.
Just tight enough to feel an increase in tension.

### Relaxation Phrases

Note how I feel as relaxation takes place.
More and more relaxed, more than ever before.
Completely relaxed, warm and relaxed.
Feel the relaxation and warmth flow through my muscles.
Throw away the tension . . . feel calm, rested.
Notice the difference (contrast) between tension and relaxation.
Relax and smooth out the muscles . . . relax to the best of my ability.
Let the tension dissolve away.
Continue letting go . . . relax . . . relax.

# NOTE

During practice sessions, say instructional phrases to yourself, *silently*. If you said the instructions out loud, you would exert effort in the muscles of your mouth and jaw—and that would interfere with complete body relaxation.

## POSSIBLE PROBLEMS

In addition to learning the rules of the program, you should be aware of difficulties that people sometimes experience. The major problems encountered by professionals when they train clients in physical relaxation are: distractions in the environment and distracting behaviors; unpleasant sensations and muscle cramps; physical tension and difficult muscles; disturbing thoughts; and sleepiness. For each of these potential problems, there *are* things you can do.

### Distractions

It goes without saying that you want to keep distractions to a minimum by finding a private and comfortable place to hold your sessions. Also keep down distracting behaviors by closely monitoring yourself and refraining from unnecessary movements. If you have a cold and find yourself coughing or sneezing, it might be a good idea to postpone a session. Arrange the environment so distracting factors are kept as low as possible.

### Unpleasant Sensations

Sensations that some people initially find uncomfortable or strange can accompany feelings of relaxation.

These may include tingling or floating sensations, dizzy feelings in your head, and small muscle spasms or jerks. These reactions are *not* unusual. In fact, they can be signals that you are becoming more relaxed. If you do feel sensations that initially seem uncomfortable, *do not move your muscles in an attempt to adjust them*. You may think that this makes your muscles feel better, but you are really only exerting effort and preventing yourself from becoming truly relaxed. If odd sensations occur, simply remain still, exert no effort. Notice how the sensations can lessen in their intensity and blend into more comfortable feelings of relaxation.

Naturally, small muscle spasms and tingling sensations are to be distinguished from uncomfortable muscle cramps. If cramps occur, it is important to reduce the time interval for tensing muscles. Alternatively, you can use less force when making the muscles tense.

### Physical Tension and Difficult Muscles

A few people who practice this program find the procedures physically arousing rather than relaxing. If you have this reaction, decrease the extent to which you actually tense your muscles during the tension phases of the program. Do so by gradually and slowly tightening a muscle until you feel the *slightest noticeable* increase in muscle tension. Then stop, do not tense up any more. Study that very small amount of tension—it will be enough to identify tension points relevant to you.

**66**

# HOW TO SCHEDULE YOUR SESSIONS

## Regular Meetings

You have already set up at least two regular appointment times each week. Starting with your next regular meeting, you can begin to work on the muscle groups in your program. Start with the muscles in your dominant hand, then go on to your arm, and continue down your list, practicing each muscle in its proper order.

Do not expect to get much further than the facial muscles during the first session. This is because you are likely to experience tension in some muscles, and these groups will be practiced as many as five times. When that happens, you cannot finish all of your muscles in a single 30-minute session.

All sessions after the first should start at the beginning of your muscle list. For example, if you complete the muscles of the hands, arms, and face during the first session, your second session, nevertheless, starts with your hands. This does not mean that you will never complete all the muscles on your list. As you get better at relaxing muscles in only two trials, you will move more rapidly from one group to the next. In that way you will eventually complete every group in a single session.

## Summary of Rules for Regular Meetings

1. Practice 30 minutes.
2. Always start with the first group on your list.
3. Practice muscles in their listed order.
4. Complete as many muscle groups as you can during the 30-minute session.

## Daily Practice Sessions

When therapists in a clinic use relaxation training, they tell their patients to practice at home twice a day for 10 to 15 minutes at a time. Since regularly scheduled sessions are equivalent to meeting with a therapist, it is important that you also practice "at home" for short periods. Convenient times for holding daily practice sessions are when you first wake up in the morning, between appointments during the day, and when you are getting ready for bed.

Do not use daily practice sessions to start new muscles. Instead, use these sessions to work on muscles that were previously practiced in your regular sessions. For example, if just the muscles in Major Group 1 were completed during your first session, you would practice only those muscles on a daily basis. With this practice, you could improve your skills and then progress more quickly to new muscle groups during your second regular session.

### Summary of Rules for Daily Practice Sessions

1. Practice 10 to 15 minutes daily.

2. Try to practice at least twice a day.

3. Never start a muscle group that has not been practiced during regular sessions.

4. Practice those muscles that need extra work.

### Use of the Log Sheets

To help you schedule sessions and keep track of your progress, there is a set of Log Sheets at the end of this chapter. These sheets provide room for recording when your sessions are held and what gets worked on in each session. The sheets will help you to keep appointments and work systematically on your program.

### GETTING READY TO BEGIN

You have already covered a lot of new material, so it may be a good idea to spend part of your next session going over it again. Before you actually practice the procedures that have been outlined, be sure you understand:

1. What muscle groups are included in your program.

2. Rules for tensing and relaxing these muscle groups.

71

3. What instructional phrases can be silently thought to yourself.

4. How to deal with possible problems.

5. How to schedule your sessions.

Once you understand these points, you can take the quiz that follows and test your mastery of the materials just read. For each question, circle the letter that represents what you think is the correct answer.

**Quiz**

1. Muscle relaxation is learned by:

    a. Trying hard to relax on your own.

    b. Alternately tensing and relaxing different muscle groups.

    c. Listening to relaxing records and thinking pleasant thoughts.

    d. Meditating about a happy thought for half-hour periods.

2. If you experience muscle cramps while tensing a muscle group, you should:

    a. Apply less force when making the muscles tight.

    b. Reduce the time interval used for tensing the group.

c. Stop practicing and go on to the next group.

d. Both a and b are correct, but c is wrong.

3. Intrusive thoughts that keep you from relaxing will probably go away on their own, but you can actively try to reduce this problem by:

a. Purposefully thinking of pleasant scenes.

b. Listening to music to distract you.

c. Holding a conversation with someone in the room.

d. There isn't anything you can do for this problem.

4. During the tension phases of your program, be sure to:

a. Make your muscles real tight so you feel them straining.

b. Let the tension spread through as much of your body as possible.

c. Focus on only one muscle group at a time and create small identifiable increases in tension.

d. Keep your eyes open so you can watch the muscles straining.

5. Imagine that you have successfully practiced the muscles in major groups 1, 2, and 3. You are now ready to begin your next regularly scheduled session. With which individual muscle group would you start this session:

a. Dominant hand.

b. Forehead.

c. Chest.

d. Thighs.

6. Daily practice sessions can help you to:

   a. Start new muscle groups.

   b. Build up your muscle strength by really tensing each group.

   c. Get better at muscles you already practiced in the regular meetings.

   d. Combine muscle practice with relaxing music.

7. The muscle exercises described in this chapter will provide you with:

   a. Easy-to-use procedures that will be helpful in any situation.

   b. Basic skills that take time to practice but will provide a foundation for developing everyday relaxation skills.

   c. Procedures that are only meant for use at home.

   d. Both b and c are true, but a is false.

Check your answers with the key below. If you missed a question, it means that you need to spend more time studying the instructional section. Only after you fully understand the materials in this chapter should you begin to practice your muscle groups. If necessary, spend your second regularly scheduled session going over these instructions.

Once you fully understand the procedures of your program, you can begin to practice the tension-relaxation exercises that have been described. What you practice on a particular day will depend, of course, on your progress in each session. During regular sessions, practice for 30 minutes the various muscle groups in their listed order. During daily practice sessions, work on especially difficult groups and increase your general skills.

One last point. If your progress is rapid, you may experience little difficulty working through all the muscle groups. You may even finish this part of your program in only two or three sessions. But finishing this quickly is unusual. Tension reactions are habits that have developed over the years. Expecting them to change overnight is unrealistic. Most of you will spend four, six, or even more regularly scheduled sessions to learn how to relax individual muscles adequately. Gradual progress is not uncommon and should not cause concern.

When you have learned to relax your muscles by practicing at home, return to this book and begin the next chapter. Chapter 3 discusses how to extend your relaxation skills so you can relax in everyday situations.


Key:
1. b
2. d
3. a
4. c
5. a
6. c
7. d

# LOG SHEET

GENERAL INSTRUCTIONS: Tense muscles for 5–7 seconds; relax them for 20–30 seconds. Tense your muscles only enough so that you can identify points of tension relevant to you. Do not overtense.

When you finish the muscles in a major group, take a "review break" and relax more fully. Practice with your eyes closed, and enjoy the relaxing effects of smooth, even breathing.

Use regular sessions to work on muscle groups in their listed order. Use daily practice sessions to improve your ability to relax already practiced muscles.

If you become uncertain about any of the procedures, read the instructional sections again

| Date | Type of Session | What Was Practiced |
|------|-----------------|--------------------|
| Jan. 10 | First Regular | Started with dominant hand and worked through facial muscles to mouth. |
| Jan. 11 | Daily Practice | Worked mostly on forehead and eyes. |
| Jan. 12 | Daily Practice | Forehead and eyes getting easier to relax. |
| Jan. 13 | Daily Practice | Reviewed hands and arms. Forehead and eyes are now easy to relax. |
| Jan. 14 | Second Regular | Started with dominant hand; this time got through to my stomach muscles — had some difficulty relaxing shoulders. |
| Jan. 15 | Daily Practice | Focused on relaxing shoulders. |

EXAMPLE — EXAMPLE — EXAMPLE — EXAMPLE

| Date | Type of Session | What Was Practiced |
| --- | --- | --- |
| | | |
| | | |
| | | |
| | | |
| | | |
| | | |
| | | |
| | | |
| | | |
| | | |

| Date | Type of Session | What Was Practiced |
|------|-----------------|--------------------|
|      |                 |                    |
|      |                 |                    |
|      |                 |                    |
|      |                 |                    |
|      |                 |                    |
|      |                 |                    |
|      |                 |                    |
|      |                 |                    |
|      |                 |                    |
|      |                 |                    |

Do not continue to the next chapter until you can relax all the muscles on your list. Be sure to keep a record of your sessions on the Log Sheets.

# 3

# Extend Your Relaxation Skills

In the last chapter, you experienced the contrast between tension and relaxation, and you learned to extend feelings of relaxation throughout your body. By practicing your exercises for 20 to 30 minutes, it should be possible now to eliminate tension and fully experience the *relaxation response*. You may recall that this is the response produced by yoga, meditation, and other relaxation programs.

Although the relaxation response is useful, it does have limitations. The numerous procedures that produce this response all require special practice sessions, during which you get away from stressful situations, assume a comfortable position, and ignore distractions. Because you often cannot do this, this relaxation program has always had a second goal—to teach you relaxation procedures that can be used throughout the day. In addition to the relaxation response, you will develop everyday *relaxation skills*.

This chapter builds upon your previous work and teaches you to relax in most any setting. The new procedures are rewarding to learn, but to learn them well, you need to work hard. Don't let your commitment to this program drop off as the weeks go by. Continue as before and hold regularly scheduled sessions. The benefits you derive will be well worth your time.

This chapter is divided into six instructional steps. Each step should be studied and practiced in order. To help track your progress, there is a new set of Log Sheets at the end of the chapter. Begin using these sheets with today's session.

## STEP 1: HOW TO COMBINE YOUR MUSCLE GROUPS

The first step in improving relaxation skills is to "combine" the muscles in each of the major groups. This means that you begin to focus attention on more than one muscle group at a time. In this way you can relax quickly while still attending to relevant tension points.

To combine your muscles, start with Major Group 1 and simultaneously tense both fists and biceps for the usual 5- to 7-second period. Then, all together, release your hold on these muscles and let them relax. Spend a good 30 to 60 seconds letting relaxation spread throughout the muscles in your hands and arms. After this period, practice for a second time the muscles in Major Group 1.

People often feel residual tension when they first combine individual groups. If this happens, you should practice in the usual way those muscles that still feel tense. For example, when combining the muscles in Major Group 1, your left biceps may remain tense during and after the relaxation periods. In that case, pay individual attention to your left biceps and practice them alone. When this part of your arm feels fully relaxed, you can go back to tensing and relaxing the entire major group as previously described.

Once you can relax, *on two consecutive trials,* the combined muscles in Major Group 1, move on to the muscles in your face, neck, and throat. Follow the same procedures for each major group until your entire body is relaxed. Notice that once you can combine the muscles in the four major groups, it will take only eight cycles of tensing and relaxing to feel totally relaxed.

Major Group 1: Hands and Arms

Major Group 2: Head, Face, and Throat

Major Group 3: Shoulders, Chest and Stomach

Major Group 4: Legs and Feet


Spend the rest of today's session learning how to combine your muscles. Between now and your next regularly scheduled session, use your daily practice sessions to sharpen this relaxation skill.

Do not continue on to Step 2 until your next regularly scheduled session. Use the Log Sheets to track your progress.

## STEP 2: ELIMINATE THE TENSION PHASES OF YOUR PROGRAM

The tension phases of your program originally helped to identify specific points of tension in your body. Now you know where to check for these points, and you know how your muscles feel when tense. So starting today, *gradually* reduce the extent to which you purposefully tense the combined muscles. In a few sessions, it will not be necessary to tighten your muscles at all. You will simply focus your attention on relevant points and see where tension exists for you.

Also start to check tension points in real-life situations. Several times a day, think about your muscle groups and see if any of them are tight. Since no one can see you do this, you can "mentally check" your muscles at work, with your family, or with friends.

Keep in mind that you are only spot-checking tension in real-life settings. Do not become frustrated if you identify tension but cannot relax it away. You will learn how to do that in the next instructional sections.

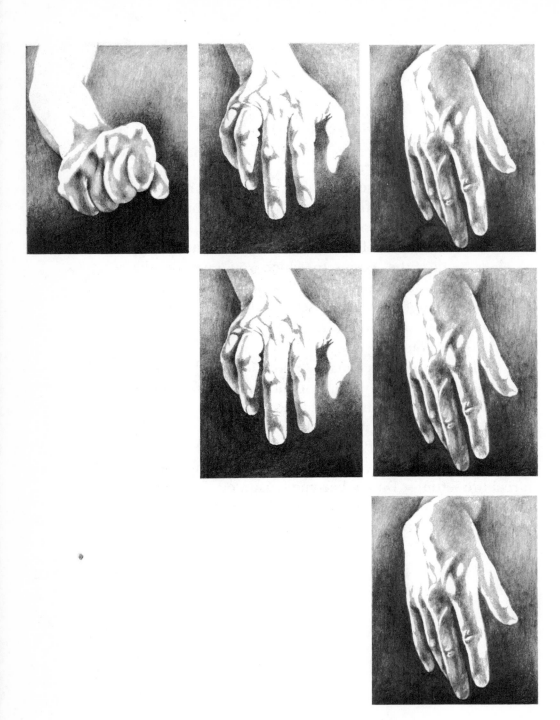

During your practice at home, begin gradually to fade out the tension phases of your program. Also spot-check your tension points several times a day. Practice these procedures for the next three or four days before proceeding to Step 3.

## STEP 3: USE OF A RELAXING WORD
## AND CONTROLLED BREATHING

You may have already developed the habit of saying to yourself words such as *calm, relax,* or *serene* during the relaxation phases of your exercises. You may have also learned to focus on the relaxing effects of exhaling smoothly and evenly. Between now and your next regular session, you will learn how to use these two factors to relax your body deeply. Then, in your next session, you will see how a relaxing word and controlled breathing provide the essential keys to the final phases of this program.

For today, first, relax all the muscles in your body by focusing on combined muscle groups, practicing individual muscles only when necessary. After your muscles are fully relaxed, focus your attention on the dominant hand. Breathe in, then out, in, then out. Each time you exhale, say to yourself a relaxing word. You can choose one of the examples given above or any other relaxing word you most enjoy using.

After breathing in and out twice, switch your attention to the next individual muscle group in the program—your dominant biceps. Repeat the procedure of breathing in and out while focusing on a relaxing word as you exhale. Then, after two breathing cycles, move to the third muscle group—your nondominant hand. Continue this sequence until you have completed all the individual muscles listed in your program.

Try this exercise now. Remember to coordinate your breathing with a relaxing word as you focus on a muscle group for two breathing cycles. After you complete this exercise, return to the instructions below.

**90**

The previous exercise helped you to become familiar with the rhythm of breathing and relaxing. You can now extend the use of a relaxing word and controlled breathing to the combined muscle groups. Start with Major Group 1 and focus your attention on the relevant tension points in your hands and arms. Keep your attention on these points for two breathing cycles. Each time you breath out, think of your relaxing word. Let this word carry you to deeper levels of relaxation. After the two breathing cycles, switch your attention to the muscles in the next major group and continue with the same procedures until all four major groups are practiced.

Between now and your next regularly scheduled session, practice the above procedures. In this way you will learn to associate deep levels of relaxation with exhaling and the use of a relaxing word. Because these procedures are enjoyable, easy to use, and *so important,* try to practice them more than once a day.

Do not continue on to Step 4 until you have spent several days practicing the use of a relaxing word and controlled breathing. Continue to keep a record of your sessions in the Log Sheets.

## STEP 4: PUTTING IT ALL TOGETHER

You are now approaching the final part of your relaxation program. Before you begin to work on this section, be sure you can:

1. Relax individual muscle groups.
2. Relax combined muscles in the four major groups.
3. Spot-check relevant tension points without purposefully tensing muscles.
4. Pair a cue word with exhaling evenly and smoothly.

Once you have developed these skills, you are ready to put them together and relax in many everyday situations. After today, it will no longer be necessary to hold regularly scheduled 30-minute sessions. Instead, you will need only to conduct one short practice session each day. Of course, since these short sessions are so easy and enjoyable, you may want to practice more than once a day. That is up to you.

Start each practice session by getting comfortable in any location of your home. Then begin to relax your body by focusing on the combined muscles in the four major groups. It only should be necessary to tense your muscles or focus on an individual group if you have trouble getting relaxed. As you focus attention on previously identified tension points, concentrate on coordinating your breathing and relaxation efforts. Also concentrate on the use of a relaxing word each time you exhale.

Although these procedures can be used in almost any situation, *restrict your efforts to your home for the next few days.* Only after you become better at rapidly relaxing at home should these skills be extended to other settings. *Be cautious and sensible.* For example, if you feel tense with large groups of people, don't immediately go out to an important party and expect to feel totally relaxed. First, try out your relaxation skills with a small gathering of three or four friends. Then progress to a situation involving several friends and one or two strangers. Later on, you can test your skills at a party or in other situations that involve many people.

Wherever you are, remember the following three-step procedure for physical relaxation. It will allow you to extend your relaxation skills to most any situation.

1. Identify tension.
2. Regulate your breathing.
3. Focus on a relaxing word as you exhale.

These procedures can be practiced at the same time that you work on Steps 5 and 6 of your program. So read the following instructional sections before you end today's session.

## STEP 5: GETTING MENTALLY RELAXED

It is not only your body that tightens up when you feel tense—your mind does too. In fact, many people find this to be a most difficult aspect of their tension. A disturbing thought may enter one's mind and "play" over and over again, making it impossible to concentrate on anything else. So quite apart from your muscles, you need to consider the mental side of relaxation.

As already mentioned in chapter 2, one approach to counteract disruptive or tense thoughts is purposefully to call to mind a pleasant image. If you keep thinking about an upsetting incident that occurred during the day, try instead to concentrate on a more relaxing scene. You can imagine yourself sitting under a tree on a beautiful spring day. Or, you can imagine a coping scene where you see yourself performing adequately in a difficult situation. For example, if you feel tense when having to go to a party or when making a request of someone, imagine yourself doing these things while remaining relaxed and *coping*. This type of scene not only provides an alternative to your original tense thoughts, but it also provides an opportunity to rehearse in your mind more desirable behaviors. Research studies by psychologists have shown that this type of "mental rehearsal" can improve performance in difficult situations. Keep this in mind as you practice imagining scenes that are incompatible with tension.

You may be thinking right now that you have already tried to change your thoughts and have found that it is not easy to do. A method that can help you to gain better control over problem thoughts is called *thought-stopping*. The basic idea behind it is easy to demonstrate. The next time you are thinking about something, pause for a moment and shout aloud the word *Stop!* You will probably want to do this when no one else is around—otherwise you may have some explaining to do! In any case, actually shout out the word *Stop* and see what happens. If you are like most people, you will temporarily lose your train of thought. For an instant, the event or situation that had been occupying your mind will be disrupted, and your mind will be "blank."

Don't worry, it isn't necessary to scream aloud everytime you want to change a thought. The only reason you should do this at least once is to demonstrate the principle that underlies thought-stopping. Once you understand this principle, you can "shout" the word Stop to yourself, *silently.*

The whole point to shouting or thinking the word Stop is that it disrupts the thought occupying your mind. During the temporary blank period that follows, you can switch your thoughts to something more pleasant. Once you switch your thoughts, the trick is to hold on to the pleasant scene or image. This may be difficult if your thoughts keep wandering back to the unpleasant event you originally wanted to change. If that happens, you should again think Stop and return to the pleasant scene. It may take several trials, and it will definitely take effort. But with repeated practice, you can gain control over unpleasant and disruptive thoughts.

How you think about pleasant events also makes a difference. For example, suppose you imagine that you are at work, feeling totally relaxed. You see yourself at your desk, working on some papers and looking rested. Unfortunately, the *real* you is passively observing the imagined scene; all the time you are outside of the scene, *you are watching yourself.*

**96**

It is far better to imagine scenes as if they are really happening, as if you are an *active participant*. Thus, you should imagine what it would be like to sit at your desk with the papers really in front of you. Feel the pen in your hand, and feel your relaxed arm resting on the desk. As you look around in your imagined scene, see the office as it actually looks from your desk. In short, you want to imagine what it is like when you *really* are at your desk. Doing this helps you to experience a scene vividly; and when an imagined scene *feels* real, it is easier to hold it in your mind.

Remember, whenever you switch your thoughts to a pleasant scene, imagine that scene as if you are actively participating in it. Keep in mind that you probably do this everytime a *tense* thought occupies your mind. When a person gets upset about work, he or she sees the office as if really there—the stomach gets the same tight feeling and the mind becomes filled with the same nervous worries. *All you need to do is to put as much energy into experiencing alternative scenes that are pleasant and enjoyable.*

Let's practice a scene to help you learn how to be an active participant in a pleasant event. Consider the following situation. You are sitting in a meadow on a beautiful fall day. Several hundred feet in front of you is a forest. Imagine this scene for a full 10 seconds (close your eyes so you can really concentrate). After you have done this, turn to the next page and see how well you did.

99

It is hoped that you just imagined yourself as an active participant. You saw the trees in front of you as if you were actually sitting in the meadow. But consider this. Did you really add details to make the scene as real as possible? Did you notice the clouds in the sky, the different shapes of the trees, the textures in the grass? Did you feel the wind and hear the leaves rustling? Was the scent of autumn in the air? In other words, did you add enough details to the scene so that all of your senses were brought to life?

Close your eyes and imagine the meadow scene a second time. This time, experience the scene to the fullest of your abilities. When you have done this, turn the page and continue with the instructions.

See the difference? Additional details bring a scene to life and make it easier to focus your attention. To demonstrate this again, practice two or three additional scenes. For example, close your eyes and imagine it is dinner time. See the members of your family sitting at the table and the food being served. Bring to mind the feelings in your stomach, the good smells of the food, and the sounds of people talking to each other. Make the scene alive so that it can surround your senses.

Throughout your program, remember this three-step procedure for mental relaxation:

1. Use thought-stopping to disrupt unpleasant thoughts.
2. Switch your attention to a pleasant or coping scene.
3. Experience your alternate scene as an active participant.

You will soon learn how to combine the above procedures with your three-step method for physical relaxation. But first study the next section to learn how to use your muscles more efficiently.

## STEP 6: DIFFERENTIAL RELAXATION

Every activity you engage in requires the use of at least *some* muscles. Even as you read this book you are using muscles in your hands, around your eyes, and possibly in your neck. Just standing still requires a degree of muscle exertion. But, although every situation requires the use of some muscles, very few require the use of *all* muscles. You may use your hands and eyes as you read this book, but there is little reason for your legs, back, or stomach to be tensed.

Check over your muscles now. Are your legs, back, and stomach fully relaxed? Probably not. Most people with tension problems forget to use their muscles efficiently. No matter what they are doing, their muscles are strained. That is why you want to practice *differential relaxation.* All that is meant by this term is that you should use your muscles efficiently—you should *differentiate* the muscles that are really needed to get a job done.

Begin today to think about differential relaxation and how you can apply this principle to all daily activities. Continue to spot check your muscles, relaxing those individual points that are not needed for the task at hand. With practice, you will start to do this automatically. When that happens, you will save body energy and reduce the uncomfortable feelings of chronic tension.

**SUMMING UP**

You are now ready to combine Steps 4, 5, and 6 of your program and extend relaxation skills to everyday situations. Remember that in real life it is unusual to feel *totally* relaxed—at least some muscles are used to accomplish even the simplest of tasks. But the previously described procedures can help you to feel *more* relaxed in most any situation. Whether you are at work, fixing dinner, studying, or driving downtown, it is always possible to focus your attention, control your breathing, and relax mentally.

During the next two weeks, use the procedures described in Steps 4, 5, and 6 and outlined below. Develop your skills first at home. Then extend your daily practice to outside situations. Do this *gradually* to avoid being overwhelmed by a highly tense situation. Also remember to use your muscles efficiently and practice differential relaxation.

| *Three-step procedure for Physical Relaxation* | *Three-step procedure for Mental Relaxation* |
|---|---|
| 1. Identify tension. | 1. Silently shout Stop. |
| 2. Control breathing. | 2. Switch your thoughts. |
| 3. Think a relaxing word as you exhale. | 3. Actively experience a pleasant or coping scene. |

When two weeks have passed, return to this book and go on to Chapter 4. In that chapter, you will be asked, "How relaxed are you now?" We will look at your daily records and current feelings to see how this program has helped you. Based on this assessment of your progress, you will plan how to develop relaxation skills further. Don't forget this important last chapter; it will be useful whether you feel totally relaxed or only slightly improved.

Practice Steps 4, 5, and 6 during the next two weeks. Keep track of your progress by using the Log Sheets. Then return to this book and work on Chapter 4.

# LOG SHEET

GENERAL INSTRUCTIONS: The six steps in this part of your program are described in Chapter 3. Follow the procedural steps as instructed and as illustrated on the following pages. If you become uncertain of any of the procedures, read the instructional sections again.

| Date | Type of Session | What Was Practiced |
|------|-----------------|--------------------|
| First Day | REGULAR | STEP 1: Combining muscle groups |
| | Daily Practice | |
| | Daily Practice | |
| | Daily Practice | |
| | REGULAR | STEP 2: Begin to eliminate the tension phases of the program. Spot-check tension daily. |
| | Daily Practice | |
| | Daily Practice | |
| | Daily Practice | |

| Date | Type of Session | What Was Practiced |
|------|-----------------|--------------------|
| | REGULAR STEP 3: | Practice the use of a relaxing word and controlled breathing. |
| | Daily Practice | |
| | Daily Practice | |
| | Daily Practice | |
| | | |
| | REGULAR STEPS 4,5,6: | Begin to practice these procedural steps. |
| | Daily Practice | |
| | Daily Practice | |
| | Daily Practice | |
| | Daily Practice | |
| | Daily Practice | |
| | Daily Practice | End of first week for practicing steps 4, 5, 6. |

| Date | Type of Session | What Was Practiced |
|---|---|---|
| | Daily Practice | Start of second week for practicing steps 4, 5, 6. |
| | Daily Practice | |
| | Daily Practice | |
| | Daily Practice | |
| | Daily Practice | |
| | Daily Practice | |
| | Daily Practice | |
| | REGULAR | Return to text and read chapter 4 — How Relaxed Are You Now? |
| | | |
| | | |
| | | |

# 4

# How Relaxed
# Are You Now?

This chapter is helpful only *after* you have completed your relaxation program. If you have reached this point, you are probably asking, "Well, have I changed? How relaxed am I now?" Your answers to these questions are important because they will help you to plan what to do next.

**SELF-ASSESSMENT**

To assess what has, and has not, changed, there are three questions to address. First ask yourself: "Am I still tense and uncomfortable in certain situations?" It may be useful at this time to check your daily records and see if any discomfort ratings have remained high. If there are situations or times during the day that continue to present problems, list them in the spaces below.

_____

_____

_____

Now ask: "Are any of my muscles still feeling tense?" Look at the Log Sheets from Chapters 2 and 3 to identify muscles that were difficult to relax during practice sessions. In addition to these muscles, there may be important areas of your body that were not covered in the original program (for example, the lower back). Think about the various muscles in your body and list any that require further practice.

_____     _____

_____     _____

_____     _____

The last question to consider in this self-assessment is: "Am I still mentally tense? (Am I repeating worried thoughts or negative self-statements over and over in my mind?") If the answer is yes, list the things you worry about in the spaces below. This will identify the specific thoughts that keep you "mentally tight."

_____

_____

_____

What has been listed on the previous pages tells you what needs to be worked on in the future. If everything has improved and there are no remaining problems, you can pretty much practice what you wish. Some people continue regular sessions at home to enjoy the relaxation response. Others find it difficult to take this time, so they employ relaxation skills only when the situation demands. Whatever you decide, keep in mind that practice is necessary to stay on top of your skills. At least once in a while, focus your attention on each muscle group and reexperience the contrast between tension and relaxation. Don't get "rusty" and drift into old tension habits.

At the opposite end of the spectrum, you may be feeling that absolutely *nothing* has changed. Although anyone who advocates a program hopes that everyone is going to feel better, there is no single treatment that provides a cure for all. So, we should discuss the possibility that you have failed.

If this program has not been a help, remember one important point: Failing at a totally self-administered program does not mean that your problem will never change. Working with a professional could lead to very different results, so don't give up. Also consider if relaxation training was really appropriate in the first place. You may remember from Chapter 1 that some tension problems result from medical ailments, which require different treatment. Other tension problems are caused by difficult situations or by people that can't be "relaxed away." If you ignored these points and proceeded with this program, you should now be more willing to see a physician or other trained professional. Get some help and properly diagnose your feelings of tension. In that way, the disappointing results from your program can lead to a positive and constructive decision for your future.

Total failures and total successes are not very common—most people fall somewhere in between. You may be more relaxed than when your program started, but particular muscle groups or situations still present problems. In such cases, there is really no reason to feel disappointed. It takes more than six or eight weeks to change long-standing tension habits. In fact, learning to have full control over physical and mental tension can be a life long project. You will get better at relaxing as the months and years go by, but there always will be room for improvement.

If tension problems do remain, it is best to continue holding regular sessions while focusing your efforts on only *one* problem at a time. This will help you to extend your relaxation skills in a planned and systematic fashion. As you work on remaining problems, remember the following points about difficult situations, muscle groups, and mental tension.

*Difficult situations:* The key to relaxing in a difficult situation is to approach that situation *gradually*. If you are tense about an approaching job interview, practice that interview with a friend. You can also gain experience by being interviewed for jobs you don't really want. If you are anxious at social gatherings, gradually increase the number of people you interact with during lunches, meetings, or parties.

The importance of gradual practice cannot be over-emphasized. As you master first one and then another situation, your general sense of confidence will increase.

*Tense Muscles:* If you find yourself really "blocked" on a particular muscle group, remember the rule about breaking the area down into more manageable sections. In this way you can more carefully focus your attention on distinct tension points that cause you problems.

For new muscle groups you should keep in mind that the key to relaxation is first to find a way to increase tension. This "backward" reasoning was the principle behind your entire program. Thus if your lower back is a problem, move around in a chair until the tightness increases. Then let go of the tightness and experience tension leaving your muscles. Never overtighten a muscle; just tense up slightly until there is a small, noticeable increase in tension. Each time a new muscle is alternately tensed and relaxed, you can extend the process of relaxation and increase your control over tension. Progress may seem slow—it can take 10, 20, 50 trials or more to relax a difficult group. But, with practice, your control over the relaxation process will improve.

*Mental Tension:* Whenever you experience mental tension, ask yourself if it is you or someone else that needs to change. Mental tension can often serve a useful function by signaling that something "out there" needs solving.

Mental tension is not useful if you simply repeat unproductive thoughts over and over and never accomplish a constructive outcome. If this type of unproductive mental tension causes you a problem, use your practice sessions in the following manner. First, let yourself become totally relaxed physically. Then employ the thought-stopping technique to disrupt problem thoughts. Immediately after doing this, concentrate your attention on the relaxing effects of exhaling. Each time that you exhale, say a relaxing word to yourself or focus on a pleasant scene. Practice these steps first at home and then work at extending your efforts to other settings.

Keep in mind that an anxious thought is like any other habit that is difficult to break. When it has been learned all too well, it will take hard work and time to change. Remember that with continued practice, your tense mind will catch up to your relaxed body.

## FINISHING UP

You have specified areas of your body that still feel tense and situations that still make you uncomfortable. Now you can continue practicing the relaxation exercises from this program. As you do this, keep your efforts focused on one problem area at a time. Also remember these two "don'ts":

*Don't be impatient*—it takes time to change tension habits.

*Don't overlook positive change*—gradual progress adds up over time.

**116**

On the next page is a Feedback Questionnaire that is easy to answer. It should take only a few minutes to complete. The information from this questionnaire can tell me how your program went and how you think this program can be improved. In this way you can contribute to future revisions of the instructions and can help others to learn to relax.

Thank you for taking the time to respond to the questionnaire.

# FEEDBACK QUESTIONNAIRE

GENERAL INSTRUCTIONS: Answer each of the following questions in terms of your own experiences. You can answer honestly because your name is not being requested. The reverse side of this questionnaire gives you mailing instructions.

1. What was your original reason for using this program? (To treat tension headaches, insomnia, general tension problems? To use as an instructional text for training students? Some other use?)

_____

_____

2. In general, how successful were you at learning to relax? Use a ten-point scale where 1 stands for "Not at all successful" and 10 stands for "Totally improved and relaxed."

| 1 | 2 | 3 | 4 | 5 | 6 | 7 | 8 | 9 | 10 |
|---|---|---|---|---|---|---|---|---|----|

NOT AT ALL
SUCCESSFUL

TOTALLY
IMPROVED AND
RELAXED

3. In the spaces below, write the weekly averages from your diary for the first, third, and last weeks of your program. Space is provided for as many as three problem situations or physical complaints. If you tracked general feelings of tension, choose three days of the week or three blocks of time during the day that were the most dificult for you.

| PROBLEM OR TIME BEING RATED | WEEK 1 | WEEK 2 | LAST WEEK |
|---|---|---|---|
| _____ | _____ | _____ | _____ |
| _____ | _____ | _____ | _____ |
| _____ | _____ | _____ | _____ |

4. Use this space to list any muscle groups or specific situations that (a) significantly improved, or that (b) still cause you problems.

| IMPROVED | STILL A PROBLEM |
|---|---|
| _____ | _____ |
| _____ | _____ |
| _____ | _____ |
| _____ | _____ |

5. Use this space for general comments. What portions of the program were helpful? What parts of the program should be improved?

## HOW TO MAIL BACK THIS QUESTIONNAIRE
Cut along the line at the right and follow Steps 1 through 4 as outlined below.

STEP 1: Fold along this line so that the top of the page folds under.

STEP 2: Fold along this line so that the bottom of the page folds under.

STEP 3:

PLACE
STAMP
HERE

To: Gerald M. Rosen, Ph.D.
The Relaxation Book
P.O. Box 25865
Seattle, WA 98125

STEP 4: Staple or tape here, and drop questionnaire in mailbox.

# ASSESSMENT FORMS

As discussed in Chapter 1, there are two different assessment forms to choose from when recording daily tension reactions. The first form allows you to track specific problem situations or specific physical complaints. The second is for monitoring general tension reactions during the course of a day. This alternate form is used when tension is not clearly associated with specific and easily identified problems.

Enough forms are provided to cover the first five weeks of your program. Make additional copies if your relaxation exercises take more time.

If you have any questions about the use of the assessment forms, refer back to the relevant instructional sections from Chapter 1.

## Assessment Form for Recording
## Physical Complaints and Problem Situations

*Instructions:*
1. Write on your form the situations or physical complaints you want to observe. Choose no more than three problems to focus on, and make at least one of your choices a "mild" problem.

2. When you experience a physical complaint or face a problem situation, indicate your degree of discomfort on a 10-point scale. Let 0 stand for *Totally Relaxed* and 10 stand for *As Tense As I Could Ever Be.*

3. After your ratings, make additional comments to clarify the nature of your physical complaint or the factors in a situation that upset you.

4. At the end of each week, compute your average ratings. Also compute averages for other relevant data (amount of medication, duration of pain, etc.).

5. If you have questions about the use of these forms, refer to pages 20-24.

ASSESSMENT FORM FOR PHYSICAL COMPLAINTS AND PROBLEM SITUATIONS

| WEEK / | PROBLEM 1 | | PROBLEM 2 | | PROBLEM 3 | |
|---|---|---|---|---|---|---|
| | Rating | Comments | Rating | Comments | Rating | Comments |
| MONDAY | | | | | | |
| TUESDAY | | | | | | |
| WEDNESDAY | | | | | | |
| THURSDAY | | | | | | |
| FRIDAY | | | | | | |
| SATURDAY | | | | | | |
| SUNDAY | | | | | | |

AVERAGES:

ASSESSMENT FORM FOR PHYSICAL COMPLAINTS AND PROBLEM SITUATIONS

| WEEK 2 | PROBLEM 1 | | PROBLEM 2 | | PROBLEM 3 | |
|---|---|---|---|---|---|---|
| | Rating | Comments | Rating | Comments | Rating | Comments |
| MONDAY | | | | | | |
| TUESDAY | | | | | | |
| WEDNESDAY | | | | | | |
| THURSDAY | | | | | | |
| FRIDAY | | | | | | |
| SATURDAY | | | | | | |
| SUNDAY | | | | | | |

AVERAGES:

ASSESSMENT FORM FOR PHYSICAL COMPLAINTS AND PROBLEM SITUATIONS

| WEEK 3 | PROBLEM 1 | | PROBLEM 2 | | PROBLEM 3 | |
|---|---|---|---|---|---|---|
| | Rating | Comments | Rating | Comments | Rating | Comments |
| MONDAY | | | | | | |
| TUESDAY | | | | | | |
| WEDNESDAY | | | | | | |
| THURSDAY | | | | | | |
| FRIDAY | | | | | | |
| SATURDAY | | | | | | |
| SUNDAY | | | | | | |

AVERAGES:

ASSESSMENT FORM FOR PHYSICAL COMPLAINTS AND PROBLEM SITUATIONS

| WEEK 4 | PROBLEM 1 | | PROBLEM 2 | | PROBLEM 3 | |
|---|---|---|---|---|---|---|
| | Rating | Comments | Rating | Comments | Rating | Comments |
| MONDAY | | | | | | |
| TUESDAY | | | | | | |
| WEDNESDAY | | | | | | |
| THURSDAY | | | | | | |
| FRIDAY | | | | | | |
| SATURDAY | | | | | | |
| SUNDAY | | | | | | |

AVERAGES:

ASSESSMENT FORM FOR PHYSICAL COMPLAINTS AND PROBLEM SITUATIONS

| WEEK 5 | PROBLEM 1 | | PROBLEM 2 | | PROBLEM 3 | |
|---|---|---|---|---|---|---|
| | Rating | Comments | Rating | Comments | Rating | Comments |
| MONDAY | | | | | | |
| TUESDAY | | | | | | |
| WEDNESDAY | | | | | | |
| THURSDAY | | | | | | |
| FRIDAY | | | | | | |
| SATURDAY | | | | | | |
| SUNDAY | | | | | | |

AVERAGES:

**Assessment Form for Recording**
**General Feelings of Tension**

*Instructions:*

1. Write in two-hour time blocks in the left-hand column of the form. Start when you usually wake up in the morning.

2. Every two hours, rate your highest degree of discomfort using a 10 point scale. Let 0 stand for *Totally Relaxed* and 10 stand for *As Tense As I Could Ever Be.*

3. Whenever your rating is high, make additional comments to clarify the situation or event that made you tense. Try to identify patterns in your ratings and comments. If it turns out that specific situations are associated with your reactions, switch to the other type of assessment form.

4. At the end of each week, compute average ratings for each day and for each time period.

5. If you have any questions about the use of these forms, refer to pages 24-27.

AVERAGES: | | | | | | | |

ASSESSMENT FORM FOR RECORDING GENERAL FEELINGS OF TENSION

WEEK _1_

| TIME/DAY | Mon. | Tue. | Wed. | Thur. | Fri. | Sat. | Sun. | COMMENTS |
|---|---|---|---|---|---|---|---|---|
| | | | | | | | | |
| | | | | | | | | |
| | | | | | | | | |
| | | | | | | | | |
| | | | | | | | | |
| | | | | | | | | |
| | | | | | | | | |
| | | | | | | | | |

Write in this left-hand column, two-hour time blocks.

AVERAGES: — — — — —

WEEK _2_    ASSESSMENT FORM FOR RECORDING GENERAL FEELINGS OF TENSION

AVERAGES: |    |    |    |    |    |    |    |

| TIME/DAY | Mon. | Tue. | Wed. | Thur. | Fri. | Sat. | Sun. | COMMENTS |
|----------|------|------|------|-------|------|------|------|----------|
|          |      |      |      |       |      |      |      |          |
|          |      |      |      |       |      |      |      |          |
|          |      |      |      |       |      |      |      |          |
|          |      |      |      |       |      |      |      |          |
|          |      |      |      |       |      |      |      |          |
|          |      |      |      |       |      |      |      |          |
|          |      |      |      |       |      |      |      |          |

Write in this left-hand column, two-hour time blocks.

AVERAGES: __ __ __

AVERAGES:

# ASSESSMENT FORM FOR RECORDING GENERAL FEELINGS OF TENSION

WEEK _3_

| TIME/DAY | Mon. | Tue. | Wed. | Thur. | Fri. | Sat. | Sun. | COMMENTS |
|----------|------|------|------|-------|------|------|------|----------|
|          |      |      |      |       |      |      |      |          |
|          |      |      |      |       |      |      |      |          |
|          |      |      |      |       |      |      |      |          |
|          |      |      |      |       |      |      |      |          |
|          |      |      |      |       |      |      |      |          |
|          |      |      |      |       |      |      |      |          |
|          |      |      |      |       |      |      |      |          |

Write in this left-hand column, two-hour time blocks.

AVERAGES:

WEEK 4

ASSESSMENT FORM FOR RECORDING GENERAL FEELINGS OF TENSION

AVERAGES:

| TIME/DAY | Mon. | Tue. | Wed. | Thur. | Fri. | Sat. | Sun. | COMMENTS |
|----------|------|------|------|-------|------|------|------|----------|
|          |      |      |      |       |      |      |      |          |
|          |      |      |      |       |      |      |      |          |
|          |      |      |      |       |      |      |      |          |
|          |      |      |      |       |      |      |      |          |
|          |      |      |      |       |      |      |      |          |
|          |      |      |      |       |      |      |      |          |
|          |      |      |      |       |      |      |      |          |

Write in this left-hand column, two-hour time blocks.

AVERAGES:

WEEK *5*

## ASSESSMENT FORM FOR RECORDING GENERAL FEELINGS OF TENSION

AVERAGES: | | | | | | | |

| TIME/DAY | Mon. | Tue. | Wed. | Thur. | Fri. | Sat. | Sun. | COMMENTS |
|----------|------|------|------|-------|------|------|------|----------|
| | | | | | | | | |
| | | | | | | | | |
| | | | | | | | | |
| | | | | | | | | |
| | | | | | | | | |
| | | | | | | | | |
| | | | | | | | | |
| | | | | | | | | |

Write in this left-hand column, two-hour time blocks.

AVERAGES: ___

# References
# and Suggested
# Reading

BENSON, H. , *The Relaxation Response*. New York: William Morrow, 1975.

COATES, T.J., and C. E. THORESEN, *How to Sleep Better: A Drug-Free Program for Overcoming Insomnia*. Englewood Cliffs, N.J.: Prentice Hall, 1977.

ROSEN, G.M., *Don't Be Afraid: A Program for Overcoming Your Fears and Phobias*, Englewood Cliffs, N.J.: Prentice-Hall, 1976.

SADLER, W.S., *Worry and Nervousness: Or the Science of Self-Mastery*. Chicago: A.C. McClurg, 1914.